I am the Lorax. I speak for the trees.

—from *The Lorax*

The editors would like to thank
DAVID GRIMALDI, PhD,
Curator, Department of Entomology, American Museum of Natural History,
for his assistance in the preparation of this book.

All photographs used under license from Shutterstock.com, with the following exceptions:
photographs courtesy Andrew Horton/USFWS, pp. 16–17; © Todd A. Ugine,
pp. 24–25; USGS Bee Monitoring and Inventory Lab, pp. 18–21.

Visit us on the Web!
Seussville.com
rhcbooks.com

Educators and librarians, for a variety of teaching tools, visit us at RHTeachersLibrarians.com

Library of Congress Cataloging-in-Publication Data is available upon request.
ISBN 978-0-593-48721-1 (trade) — ISBN 978-0-593-48722-8 (lib. bdg.)

Printed in the United States of America

10  9  8  7  6  5  4  3  2  1

First Edition

# Hug a Bug

## How YOU Can Help
## Protect Insects

by Bonnie Worth
illustrated by Aristides Ruiz

Random House 🏠 New York

I am the Lorax,
and I've come here to say
that some bugs need our help
(and they need it TODAY!).

The world swarms with bugs.
It might boggle some minds
when I say there are well
over one million kinds!

When I say the word BUGS,

some people cry, PESTS!

They slap them or zap them

or poison their nests.

But bugs are important.

In fact, I insist . . .

. . . without bugs our world
simply could not exist!

Some bugs pollinate,
helping make fruits and seeds,
while others eat pests
and still others eat weeds.

Some bugs are the food
that helps animals thrive.
(It's a balanced bug diet
that keeps them alive.)

Some bugs need your hugs
because they're dying out.
These bugs are the ones
I am talking about.

HUG
-a-
BUG

Monarch's eggs are glued
to the leaves of milkweed.
Larvae hatch, and those leaves
provide food that they need.

As a larva grows bigger,
it sheds skin, like this.

It then clings to a leaf
to form a chrysalis.

About fifteen days later,
come back and you'll see,
the adult emerges—
in its majesty!

When temperatures drop,
monarchs gather and swarm,
flying two thousand miles south
to a forest that's warm.

Forest habitats have
sadly shrunken away.
And some people kill milkweed
with a poisonous spray.

What with milkweed spraying
and habitat chopping,
the numbers of monarchs
are steadily dropping.

Why is butterfly loss
such a huge, big deal?

13.

The effect on us humans
is realer than real!

I'm telling you this
for your information,
bugs like the monarch
perform cross-pollination.

pollen

Bugs transfer pollen
from flower to flower,
giving the flower
its reproductive power!

stamen

pistil

Bugs help the flowers
spread and flourish.
Flowers make fruits
and veggies that nourish.

Skippers get their name
because they skip to and fro,
sipping flower nectar.
They pollinate as they go.

On rich prairie grass
skipper larvae grow fat.
But prairie is now scarce—
and I'm sorry for that.

Cities and farms now stand
where prairie grass waved.
Dakota skippers may die out
if they are not saved.

17

Let me now speak
for the dear bumblebees.
They live in a nest
in small bee colonies.

The nest is so crowded
that when it gets hot,
it needs air-conditioning,
bee-lieve it or not.

Next to the door
those bumblebees there
flap their wings very fast,
and it cools off the air.

**Did you know?**
Bumblebees are important pollinators
of tomatoes and berries and potatoes.

QUEEN
BEE

The queen lays her eggs
in the colony nest.
The larvae eat pollen.
It's what they digest!

larvae

Bumblebees are all fuzzy.
That fur coat surely pays!
They can still make their rounds
on the coldest of days.

When weed spray kills flowers
in the bumblebees' space,
there's no food for the larvae.
No pollination takes place.

**Did you know?**
When you eat honey, you are eating
concentrated flower nectar.

Some bees hang in crowds,
but as I have found,
digger bees are loners
in nests underground.

In bare, sandy spots
in your park or backyard,
you may spot digger nests
if you look very hard.

**Did you know?**
Most bees are solitary and do not live in colonies.

Weed killer on lawns?

Not the wise thing to do.

It kills pollinating

digger bees, too.

These ladybugs here
all have nine pretty spots.
(You can't see them all
but they're there—nine black dots!)

They are very good friends
to the gardeners I meet
because they like aphids
as a tasty treat.

The praises of aphids
are seldom sung,
since they eat garden plants
when they're tender and young.

The antennae on an American
burying beetle's head
can smell a small critter
the moment it's dead.

This beetle lays eggs
beneath the buried beast.
When the larvae hatch out,
it is their time to FEAST!

EGGS

That is SO GROSS—
even for me, I confess—
but a jim-dandy way
to clean up nature's mess.

LARVAE

Tiger beetles can rip.

They are such speedy guys!

They pounce on caterpillars,

nab midges, gnats, flies.

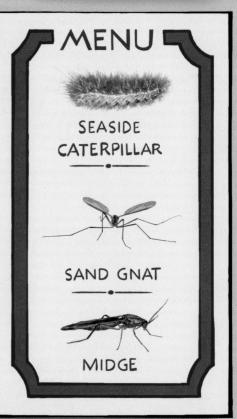

When these beetles eat pests,

then we don't need to spray.

They are small, but they offer us

BIG help this way.

They bury their eggs
in the sandy seaside.
Now beach houses crowd
them, this can't be denied.

These hovering flies
sip nectar from flowers,
which they pollinate
during their busy hours.

Some flower flies eat aphids
and pests that eat crops.
Their usefulness to farmers,
you see, never stops.

But when flies are endangered
by human habitation,
say hello to those pests
and goodbye, pollination!

Hine's emerald dragonfly,
if I understand right,
spends much of its adult
life feeding in flight.

**Did you know?**
Dragonflies eat flying insects, like biting
flies, gnats, and mosquitoes.

In wetlands, it lays eggs.
And when nymphs hatch out,
they feed on wee worms
and bugs all about.

But we're losing wetlands
alarmingly fast.
And without them these beauties,
I fear, will not last.

EGGS          NYMPHS

I speak for the bugs,
for the bugs have no voice.
But I'm telling you now
that you DO have a choice.

You can speak for them, too,
and speak from your heart.
Learning what you can do
is the best way to start.

UNLESS someone like YOU
cares a whole awful lot,
these bugs won't survive.
No, they simply will not.

# How YOU Can Help!

CONEFLOWER

First, you can plant
a garden to please
our pollinator helpers:
butterflies and bees.

BUTTERFLY WEED

BEE BALM

YARROW

POPPY

COSMOS

Remind your folks
there is simply NO WAY
they should use bug poisons
or nasty weed spray.

Don't have room to garden?
Then keep in mind that
there are groups to support
who protect habitat.

SUNFLOWER

BORAGE

ASTER

LAVENDER

ANEMONE

CALENDULA

To help these groups,
you can, without fail,
raise funds from a lemonade
stand or bake sale.

Bugs suffer from
global warming, for sure.
Burn less fossil fuel
and you'll help with their cure.

click!

Don't ride in the car
if you can walk there or jog.
Try hard not to be
an electricity hog.

**MASON**

**LEAF-CUTTER**

With an adult's help, make a house for solitary nesters like these— the mason, leaf-cutter, or yellow-faced bees.

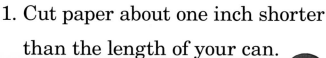

You will need:

- paper
- scissors
- can
- pencil

- tape
- glue
- toilet paper rolls
- wire or string

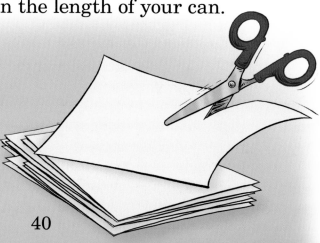

1. Cut paper about one inch shorter than the length of your can.

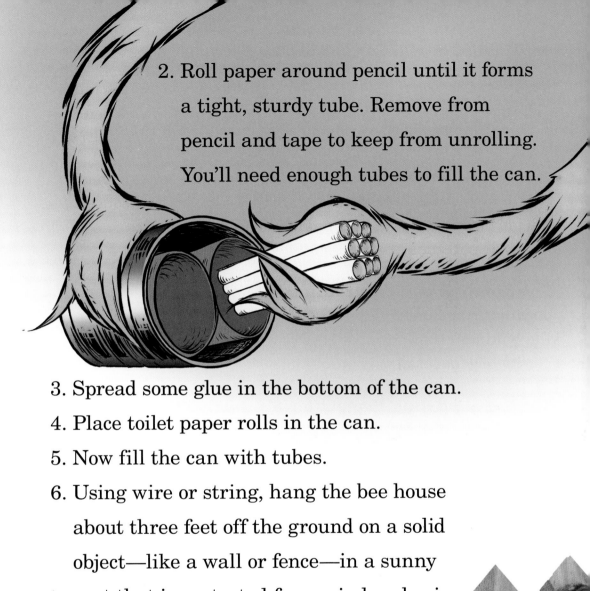

2. Roll paper around pencil until it forms a tight, sturdy tube. Remove from pencil and tape to keep from unrolling. You'll need enough tubes to fill the can.

3. Spread some glue in the bottom of the can.

4. Place toilet paper rolls in the can.

5. Now fill the can with tubes.

6. Using wire or string, hang the bee house about three feet off the ground on a solid object—like a wall or fence—in a sunny spot that is protected from wind and rain.

# For More Information

Just like the Lorax, YOU can be a caring community scientist. Get involved in the effort to save threatened and endangered insects. You can learn more by checking out these websites:

**BugGuide.Net** is an online community of insect enthusiasts that offers pictures, identification, and information concerning a wide variety of bugs and spiders of North America.
bugguide.net/node/view/15740

The **Bumblebee Conservation Trust** is a science-led organization committed to the conservation of bumblebees in the wild and their habitat restoration.
bumblebeeconservation.org

The **Lost Ladybug Project** invites children to work with scientists in performing ladybug observation, gathering data, compiling surveys, and searching for sightings of this rare and valuable insect.
lostladybug.org/about.php

**The Monarch Joint Venture** organization encourages adults and children to participate in the study and protection of the monarch butterfly.
monarchjointventure.org/get-involved/study-monarchs-community -science-opportunities

From whipping up a paste to attract moths to building a hummingbird bath, the **Nature Conservancy** offers lots of fun stuff to do that benefits the pollinators in your neighborhood.
nature.org/en-us/magazine/magazine-articles/pollinator-paradise/

The **Pollinator Partnership** is the largest organization in the world devoted to the protection and promotion of bug life. In addition to information about different pollinators, you'll find lots of educational materials, plus activities to do at home and in the classroom.

pollinator.org/learning-center/education

The **World Wildlife Federation** has created a site geared to giving teachers and parents resources to teach children about the natural world.

worldwildlife.org/teaching-resources

The **Xerces Society** takes its name from the now-extinct Xerces blue butterfly. Their mission is to prevent the future disappearance of other threatened or endangered invertebrates. Take the pollinator protection pledge to bring back the pollinators by sticking to the society's core values: "grow pollinator-friendly flowers, provide nest sites, avoid pesticides, and spread the word."

xerces.org/pollinator-conservation/pollinator-protection-pledge

# Glossary

**Antennae:** Feelers on the heads of insects that may sense smell, sound, taste, or vibration.

**Aphid:** A bug that feeds by sucking sap or juice from plants.

**Chrysalis:** A hardened case protecting a butterfly or moth in the larval stage.

**Digest:** To break down food for nutrition.

**Habitat:** The natural home for a plant, animal, or insect.

**Larva:** The wingless stage of life of many insects.

**Nectar:** The sugary liquid made by flowers and plants designed to attract pollinating insects and animals.

**Nymph:** An insect whose wings have not yet developed.

**Pistil:** The part in the center of a flower that produces the seed.

**Pollen:** The fine powder produced by plants that's needed to make seeds.

**Pollination:** Brought about by wind, rain, animals, and insects, the process of sharing pollen by the same types of plants that causes them to reproduce.

**Stamen:** The part of the flower that produces pollen.

**Wetlands:** Natural areas, like swamps, bogs, or marshes, that hold lots of water and host a variety of plant, animal, and insect life.

# Index

Encourage a love of nature
and respect for the environment in children of ALL ages
with these books featuring Dr. Seuss's Lorax!